GRANDPA & GRANDMA
GONOPOLIS

MAKING DOUGH ON THE FARM

by Uncle Hyggly

In loving memory of Margaretta.

WOUNDED COOT *Greetings*
2001 Killebrew Drive, Suite 100
Bloomington, Minnesota 55420

Other books by Uncle Hyggly:

Mr. Gonopolis And His 12 Holsteins – *A Christmas Story*

Copyright © 1986 Charles R. Dewey
All rights reserved
First printing November 1986

Uncle Hyggly (Charles R. Dewey)
   Grandpa & Grandma Gonopolis — Making Dough on the Farm
   First Edition
   Bloomington, Minnesota

ISBN 0-935583-02-5

Over the river and through the woods,
   to Grandfather's farm we went.
Our mom would go shopping, she would not be stopping
   'til all of her money was spent.

We eagerly rode down that old gravel road
as our mom drove as fast as a flash.
As the wheels hit the holes from the seats we arose
things were jumping all over the dash!

A warm autumn day and the sweet smell of hay
if it got better than this, who would think it?
And wouldn't you guess the milk would be so fresh
that you'd slap it before you could drink it?

A kiss we got threw, said our mom "Tool-la-roo"
    as she sped off in search of the stores.
My little brother went with our grandmother
    as I ran to help Grandpa with chores.

With Tad in the kitchen my grandma was mixin',
  a pan full of fluffy bread dough.
With love and affections she followed directions
  and measured the portions just so.

"These eggs aren't too new, but I guess they will do,"
   she said as she gave one a click.
And when the egg broke she expected a yolk
   but instead what she got was a chick!

The chicks multiplied with the more eggs she tried
— the carton had turned a bit fowl.
Stuck with a case full of egg on the face,
Grandma herded them off with a towel.

Tad could not wait for that dough to inflate,
  his impish impatience increased.
He had ants in his pants as he did a small dance
  and then dumped in the whole jar of yeast!

He watched with big eyes for the dough now to rise
but it sat there. . . AND sat there . . . AND sat!
So he sighed, ran away to continue his play
when the dough slowly rose from its vat!

He turned on the faucet and dug through the closet
then <u>jumped</u> when he heard a loud **SNAP!**
From the third cupboard door that was down by the floor
Grandma pulled out a mouse in a trap!

Grandma took that poor mouse right on out of her house,
  as Tad wondered what else lurked below.
Amongst the pans and the pots and the toasters and clocks
  just creeping and crawling <u>*real*</u> *slow!*

Maybe he would explore, finding large **DINOSAUR**
that he'd tame to help plow Grandpa's fields.
And with their great size they could help fertilize
and quadruple our grandfather's yields!

Or maybe robots would leap out from those pots,
    threatening evil and dread.
But our grandfather's tools would take care of those fools
    and transform them to combines instead!

His jaw set defiant and with Ol' Reliant
(his toy gun made out of a broom),
With big steps he crept toward the demons that slept
down below in that <u>Cupboard Of Doom!</u>

SUDDENLY! — a deep roar --that tore loose the whole door
—and great clouds of sawdust arose!
And the next thing he saw was a large clawing paw
which then took a swipe at his toes!

He bounded upstairs as a fur-rocious bear
barely missed him with each lunging nip.
His heart filled with fear as that hot breath grew near
and his underwear slipped off his hip!

He cleared the last rung but his stocking got hung
    on a nail jutting up in the hall.
There were paws all around as a darkness came down
    but just then he heard Grandmother's call.

She said "What's dis yelling?" Her voice was compelling,
it lifted Tad out of his fog.
When he shook his head what he saw there instead
was just Grandpa's silly old dog!

My brother giggled as Mort's tail wiggled,
Mort gave him a slobbering lick.
With grandma's defenses he retrieved his senses
as well as Mort fetches his stick.

Grandma let loose a snort that did startle poor Mort
     as she laughed "Dere are no monsters here!
Yah see, little Tad, It is all in yer h'ad"
     but a sound blustered up from the rear.

Then a raw, swelling smell waffled up the stairwell
swallowing steps as it rose.
A new beast was unleashed by that jarful of yeast
— a monsterous <u>BLOB</u> made of dough!

It gurgled and oozed right on up to their shoes
and it slupped and it slurped as it slipped.
Grandma grabbed the old broom as it came 'cross the room
leaving lamps and the furniture tipped!

She gave it a whack but that dough leaped right back
puffing bigger and bigger, until,
— It grew yet some more filling up the whole floor
and then pushed them right out on the sill!

"Ole!" Grandma cried to my grandpa outside
"You had better get here on da double."
Her Norwegian reserve was beginning to swerve
when she told him "Our buns are in trouble!"

With pitchfork held high and a fierce battlecry
my grandfather plunged into action.
A mountain of dough swelling out of control
did not fit in his plans for expansion.

He stabbed it and stuck it without any luck it
fell back, but then grew even bigger!
To help stem that tide I stood right at his side
hacking at it with teeth from the digger!

Try as we might we were losing the fight and
my grandfather found it alarming.
It was the first time you know, he had been in the dough
in the sixty-three years he'd been farming!

Suddenly, the air stilled and then filled with a chill
as a cold front was now quickly dropping.

It was just what we kneaded — *the dough now receded*
and it sounded like cereal popping!

That dough loosened it's hold, shrinking back from the cold
as the temperature kept right on falling.
But as the dough hurried my grandpa looked worried
and soon to his cows he was calling:

"Moove e'fery hoof now get under da roof now,"
my grandfather raised the alarm.
It was no longer warm, now a great winter storm
was moving right in on the farm!

Bossie and Bessie and Hulda and Jessie
followed Sally and Gertrude and Mary.
Eleven were all that did answer his call
of the twelve in my grandfather's dairy!

Somewhere out in the frost our poor Sigrid was lost
but the storm was now blowing real hard.
"Ve must pray she's okay," I heard Grandfather say,
"For ve cannot go out in dah yard."

Grandpa gave me a smile, we were safe for awhile
just as long as his old barn would take it.
Then the wind *driving hard* from the north *through the yard*
started to <u>shimmy</u> and <u>shammy</u> and <u>shake</u> it . . .

The gusts grew yet stronger and it wasn't much longer
 'til it leaned like the Tower of Pisa.
And then it leaned MORE, folding down towards the floor
 and traveling without any visa!

Grandpa cried to the swine, "Get yoursel'fes in a line
    for ve got us some verk to be done!
Get your tails out dere spinnin', this war ve'll be winnin'
    Yust do it and I'll owe ya one!"

Those curly propellers on each of those fellers
    first spittered, then sputtered, then rotated.
I felt a brisk breeze flowing fast past my knees
    as that pig pressure system gestated!

They gave it their all and they righted the wall
but it still was not time for elation.

The wind held its course, hit the barn with a force
that blew it right off its foundation!

The wind did not yield , we slid 'cross the field
skidding 'cross snow-freckled loam.
My grandfather groused "If dis had been dah house
ve could call it a mobile home!"

Grandpa looked out at our runaway's route
squinting to see through the snow.
Straight dead ahead was the Peterson spread
—and right through their house we would go!

43

Without missing a beat Grandpa jumped to his feet
and clutching his old fishing pole,
To the roof he was climbing, with pretty strange timing --
it was late in the season to troll!

44

Perched on the crest with some 20 lb. test
he casted and snagged an old sign.
His rusty old reel spewed forth with a squeal
there was plenty of drag on the line.

Grandpa held tight as it gave him a fight
up there on the roof standing tall.
His plan was now working, we stopped without jerking
a foot from the Peterson's wall!

"Peterson" Grandpa said as my face turned to red
      and he climbed off the roof from his labors,
"In all of mankind I would bet'cha you'd find
      dere haf nef'er been two closer neighbors!"

WHOOSH

47

When the weather improved we got the barn moved,
as the animals gave it a heave.

The sun was now fading, my grandma was waiting
(and the Petersons thought we should leave).

On the path we had chosen we found Sigrid frozen
as stiff as a fish on the ice.
I thought this was the end of my black and white friend
but the words from my grandpa were wise:

Grandpa said, "Stop your frettin', you see what I'm bettin'
    a thawing is all that she takes."
Sigrid quivered and shivered and then she delivered
    a bucket of frosty milkshakes!

Grandpa said we should stay 'til the very next day
'cause the roads were all blocked by the storm.
While outside it flurried, to the table we hurried
while the buns Grandma baked were still warm.

We chewed and we chewed and we chewed and we chewed
then we chewed and we chewed yet some more.
That bread was unleaven, we chewed until seven
and then rested our jaws, which were sore!

Grandpa put down his cup when our mom called him up
to make sure we were all safe from harm.
And he said "How are you? Oh, no, not much is new,
yust a regular day on dah farm."

Grandma tucked us in bed when our prayers were all said
and I got a small peck on the cheek.
But it wasn't Grandmother or even my brother
but a kiss from a baby chick beak!

Grandma turned out the light and Tad's fancy took flight
when he found a great lump in his bed.
He stared at the ceiling and what he was feeling
was hope that the bear had been fed!